IMAGES
of America

DETROIT'S POLONIA

ST. ALBERTUS CHURCH EXTERIOR AND INTERIOR. Founded in 1872, St. Albertus was the first Polish Roman Catholic church in Detroit. It was the base for many Polish immigrants in the late 19th and early 20th centuries. The church was closed in 1990. St. Albertus is an official Michigan historic site, and the Polish American Historic Site Association was formed to oversee its maintenance and restoration. (AFSLM.)

IMAGES
of America

DETROIT'S POLONIA

Cecile Wendt Jensen

ARCADIA
PUBLISHING

Published by Arcadia Publishing
Charleston, South Carolina

Library of Congress Catalog Card Number: 2005934537

For all general information contact Arcadia Publishing at:
Telephone 843-853-2070
Fax 843-853-0044
E-mail sales@arcadiapublishing.com
For customer service and orders:
Toll-Free 1-888-313-2665

Visit us on the Internet at www.arcadiapublishing.com

On the cover: **DYNGUS DAY.** "Smigus Dyngus!" is the nonsense name of both the custom and the cry of the participants. The ritual follows Easter, and the dousing with water represents rain for the land and fertility for the participants. It is accompanied by a switching with willow branches. A tradition brought from Polish villages, the practice was captured by a *Detroit News* photographer in the early 20th century. (The Detroit News Collection/Walter P. Reuther Library, Wayne State University.)

CONTENTS

ACKNOWLEDGMENTS

My premiere thanks to Seamus Murphy, better known as Jim Jensen, for selecting a girl of Polish heritage as his wife in 1972 and for supporting my genealogical research.

Thank you, my dear parents, Frank Wendt and Elizabeth Przytulska and grandparents Anthony Przytulski, Cecilia Wojtkowiak, Frank Wendt, and Agata Zdziebko for giving me my Polish heritage.

I extend my thanks to Jim Tye and Ken Merique. They are noted researchers and writers who have contributed unique photographs and offered collegial guidance in the development of *Detroit's Polonia*. Their research and writing enhance *Detroit's Polonia* throughout. I was also given wholehearted support by Joe and Betty Guziak.

A photographic outline for the book was suggested by William Gorski's work from the 1980s, now part of the J. William Gorski collection at the Archives of Michigan. I also appreciate the use of his unpublished tombstone portraits.

Images are used from the archive collections of the following: the Archives of the Felician Sisters, Presentation of the Blessed Virgin Mary Province, Livonia, Michigan (AFSLM), Sister Elaine, archivist; and the Detroit New Collection/Walter P. Reuther Library, Wayne State University (DNC/WRL), Thomas Featherstone, archivist.

Family albums used for the creation of this book include those of: Lucille Rozman Dean (LRD), Cheryl Funk (CF), J. William Gorski (JWG), Robert and Camille Jankowski (RCJ), Valerie Warunek Koselka (VWK), Kenneth A. Merique (KAM), Brundirks/Owiesny (DBO), Genevieve Marie (Pruss) Dunneback (GPD), Don Samull (DS), Jann Soltis (JLS), Cecilia (Gasiorek) Suchyta (CGS), Kathleen Labudie Szakall (KLS), John Szaroleta (JS) , James Tye (JT), Patrick J. Topolewski family (PTF), Joseph (Wojtkowiak) Voight (JV), Arthur and Magdalene (Sajewicz) Wagner (AMW), Frank and Elizabeth (Przytulska) Wendt (FEW), Bernadine Mormol Wendt (BMW), Thomas Wozniak (TW), and Frank Zynda (FZ).

INTRODUCTION

The vestiges of the first Polish communities in Detroit are in rapid decline. Upward mobility, World War II, expressways, and suburbia encouraged the succeeding generations to disperse. This book is a collection that brings a Polonian album together so future generations can read about their legacy. It is ironic that we can travel to Poland today and attend mass in the church that our great-grandparents were married in, but so many of the churches our parents were wed in have been closed or torn down.

The flow of immigrants from Poland began with Kashubs and Prussian Poles. Several factors helped make them the first immigrants, including the railroad infrastructure in the German partition. Prussian military conscription was something ethnic Poles wanted to avoid. Soon the Galicians and Russian Poles followed. It was a challenge to come from the more economically depressed and less accessible region, yet Catholics, Jews, and Evangelical Poles sailed for the United States.

The geographic boundaries easily divide the earliest east-side community from the west-side community. Descendants today still define themselves as Eastsiders or Westsiders. Jim Tye's research documents that as early as 1872, there were some 300 Polish families in Detroit. These Polish pioneers organized the first Polish parish in Detroit in 1872, St. Albertus, located at St. Aubin and Canfield. The area they occupied was bounded by Canfield, Garfield, Orleans, and St. Aubin. By 1882, the Polish population in Detroit had increased to 1,190 families, and in 1885, the Polish population of the city was estimated at 22,000. Due to immigration, the number of Poles in the city climbed to 35,000 by 1892, 48,000 by 1900, and over 120,000 in 1903.

The geographic divides defined the early communities, but more things bound them together. Family, language, and religion were cornerstones for the immigrants. Many aspects of the village were brought with them. The priest had a strong presence as a religious and community leader. The nuns were a new concept to schooling. In their villages, there was little education, except during the winter months, and Bismarck's Kulturkampf suppressed Polish language study. The evolution of bilingual techniques developed by Jozef Dabrowski and the Felician Sisters was a hybrid of the Old and New Worlds.

This book is a community family album. The images were collected from families' collections as well as archives. It is a visual documentation of the pioneers and their hope for a better life. What would they think? The descendants of Piotr Wojtkowiak are now the Voights. The Stefan Wojtkowiak line are now Kowiaks, and the Tomasz Zdziebko family has branched out to Japkos, Jepkos, and Zipkos. The descendants have been woven into the fabric of America.

The miners and lumberjacks from Calumet, Ironwood, and Laurium became cigar makers and railroad car and stove builders. The workers carting wood became teamsters and union members. Car building no longer meant Michigan railcars but Ford, GM, and Chrysler. They dug the sewers, laid the wooden sidewalks, and set up breweries. The women created a legacy of sewing, laundry, and millinery shops. Tye remarks that the Polish settlers were self-sufficient, establishing their own shops, bakeries, hardware stores, breweries (Zynda Brewery on Canfield near Russell), as well as their own farmers' market, the Chene-Ferry Market. There you could buy a porker on the hoof, a live chicken, duck, or turkey, or fresh produce. In 1916, Joseph Witkowski established one of his clothing stores at the corner of Chene and Adele.

Habits learned in Poland were practiced in America. The Polish homes in Detroit were decorated with pictures of their name day saints, a custom brought with them from their Polish villages. Foods like spicy kielbasa and tangy sauerkraut were made from old recipes and included in traditional holiday meals like the Wigilia dinner. The Easter Swieconka basket included ham and kielbasa, babka, and decorated eggs (*pisanki*). There was usually a Paschal Lamb or *Baranek* made of butter. Some Detroit families maintained chicken coops and kept goats and horses in the yard. Tending a few animals reminded them of their old livelihood and bridged the transition from farmer to city dweller.

Polish immigrants also moved into the political arena. Three Michigan lieutenant governors have been of Polish heritage: Leo Nowicki, T. John Lesinski, and John D. Cherry. John Dingell (Dziegelewicz) (1894–1955) and his son John (1926–) both served as Michigan congressmen for Michigan's 15th district.

The community and photography moved in tandem. This collection moves from formal, stoic portraits to World War II 35-millimeter instant images. The photographs introduce us to pioneers who left all they knew and the little they had to take a chance on America.

The Poles heeded a notice at the Ford plant written in Polish, which closed with "Learn to Read and Write English." The Poles did that—and more.

ST. CASIMIR INTERIOR. Shown here is St. Casimir, which was located on the corner of Twenty-third and Myrtle Streets from 1883 to 1990. Leo A. Bonish took this photograph during the church's golden jubilee in 1932. (TW.)

One

PIONEERS

PRIESTS, NUNS, AND FAMILIES

OLD AND NEW. This *Detroit News* photograph was indexed under "foreign colonies," but the double portrait is a harbinger of the assimilation that the pioneer families would experience. The mother's head is covered with a peasant scarf, but the daughter, taller and more urbane, wears a stylish hat and dress. (DNC/WRL.)

MOTHER MARY MONICA SYBILSKA (1824–1911).
This is a photograph of the first Mother Provincial of the Felician Sisters in America (1881). Fr. Jozef Dabrowski advised them to travel in secular clothing when they entered Prussia because of Bismarck's religious intolerance. The motherhouse in Detroit, Michigan, was established in 1881. Father Dabrowski installed his printing press on the ground floor of the convent. Mother Sybilska is interred at Mount Elliott Cemetery. (AFSLM.)

SR. MARY CAJETAN JANKIEWICZ, CONGREGATION OF THE SISTERS OF ST. FELIX CANTALICE (1839–1907). Born in Warsaw, Poland, on February 26, 1839, Sister Jankiewicz was born to an affluent and cultured family. She entered the Felician Congregation in 1867 with a teaching degree and several years of experience. With Father Dabrowski, she drew up the first school curriculum for parochial schools and a system for the professional training of future religious teachers. Sister Jankiewicz died in 1907 during a retreat, and her remains were buried in Polish soil. (AFSLM.)

Fr. Jozef Dabrowski (1842–1903).
Father Dabrowski was the Polish
community's Renaissance man. He
was banished from Poland for his role
in the 1863 uprising. He established
the Polish Seminary and invited the
Felician Sisters to the United States.
He was the director of the convent and
girls orphanage. Katharine Wojtkowiak,
a ward, remembered when he gathered
them in a room and cheered "Electra,"
after lighting the first electrical lightbulb
in the convent. (AFSLM.)

**Raising the Roof on
St. Albertus.** The
American flag was raised
as the steel framework of
the school building was
completed. It was the third
school building to be built. It
still stands behind the church
on Canfield Street. (DS.)

11

RECZEK FAMILY. The Reczek family went to the portrait studio soon after arriving in Detroit. The father looks *goral*. He is dressed in the traditional highlander garb, which included white, tight woolen trousers embroidered with *parzenica* and a leather belt. (CF.)

AUGUST KULWICKI FAMILY. August Kulwicki, brother of Martin, assisted in his brother's funeral business. Martin had established the first Polish funeral home in Detroit in 1878, located at the southeast corner of St. Albin and Willis, across from St. Albertus Church. It is nice to see a family portrait with three generations and a beautiful smile on Mary Kulwicki Armknecht's face. She is holding Eleanor Armknecht, later Mrs. Arthur Distler. (KAM.)

MARY KROK. Few albums have photographs of ancestors dressed in the regional clothing. Mary is photographed here in her Poznañian-style blouse and her beads. It is not known if the rich red necklace was made from fine coral or red wooden beads, but one can see it was the finishing touch to the outfit. Mary's daughter Katherine married Andrew Sitek. (CF.)

ZYNDA FAMILY AROUND 1900. Brewer John Zynda was a high-profile brewer, politician, and benefactor in Detroit. Pictured from left to right are the following: (front) Aloysius; (first row) Charles, mother Augustine (née Eichler), Rose, father John Sr., Leo; (second row) Joe, Paulina, Helen, Anna, and John Jr. (FZ.)

CITY MARKET. This *Detroit News* photograph is dated October 18, 1912. It is entitled "Scenes Taken at Market." The photograph brings to mind the Eastern, Central, Campus Martius, Chene, and Ferry Streets markets where Detroiters shopped. On the shelves are kitchen staples, including Kellogg's cereal. (DNC/WRL.)

COLLECTING COAL. Many families have stories about the family members picking up coal along the railroad tracks. Children as well as adults hunted for the lumps of coal that fell off the cars. Sometimes misfortune followed with children, falling ill after being out in the rain and cold or being caught under the wheels. (DNC/WRL.)

HELEN'S HAT. Helen and her mother, Antonina Ostrowska, wear fashionable outfits for their portrait. For many women, being a milliner or dressmaker was a better opportunity than being in domestic service because the work could be done at home. Many women could make a dress from looking at the store version and cutting their own patterns from brown paper bags. (FEW).

CLEAN SWEEP. Humble but necessary work was had as an employee of Detroit's Public Works Department. Many a Pole supported his family during the Depression doing this job. (DNC/WRL.)

DEEP IN THE MINES. For more than 100 years, hundreds of Detroiters made their living by mining the salt used for deicing roads, ice cream, and cattle licks. Detroit has one of the world's largest rock-salt mines 1,200 feet beneath Detroit and other Wayne County communities. Larry Lewandowski's great-uncle John worked for the Pennsylvania Salt Manufacturing Company. (DNC/WRL.)

SALT MINERS. There are 50 miles of roads in the salt mines, and some are as wide as four-lane highways. Operations began in 1896. Workers and equipment were lowered through a five-by-six-foot shaft. The temperature was a constant 58 degrees Fahrenheit and 55 percent humidity. (DNC/WRL.)

16

ICE MAN, MAY 17, 1911. Many Detroiters remember the iceman's delivery. While he was bringing the block of ice into the kitchen to set in the icebox, mischievous boys and girls would try and sneak ice chips off the truck, only to hear the sharp words of the driver when they were discovered. (DNC/WRL.)

STOVE MOLDERS. Working in the dark, hot foundry of the stove companies was a taxing but a steady job for many immigrants. A quick review of 1900 and 1910 census records shows that this was a common job for many Poles. (DNC/WRL.)

GRANDMA IN DETROIT. Rosalia Kronkowski (1853–1921) seems to be in her element in the backyard. While the background could easily be mistaken for a farm in Poland, it is believed to be the yard at 220 Williams Street (now 3746). She and her husband, Michael, arrived in the United States in 1873. (TW.)

RODZINA ZYNDA. John Zynda, like many pioneers, did not sever ties with his Polish village. One of his visits to his village of Koscierzyna, Kreis Berent, was recorded in this family photograph. The men of the family are front and center, but two women are seen peaking out of the doorway with smiles on their faces. (FZ.)

18

BARBARA ORLOWSKA LERCH CIESZYNSKA (1815–1876). Barbara was the daughter of Jan Orlowski and Katarzyna Dudek. She was the matriarch of the Lerch/Lark family of Detroit that has more than 1,000 descendants. This photograph was taken at F. G. Lutge, located on Monroe Avenue, in 1875. (KAM.)

BUSHA'S BABUSHKA. The woman hurries along a wooden fence, possibly in front of a church. The barefoot boy's short pants contrast with the woman's dark clothing. Where she is heading is not known, but in the close community, brother and sister and nieces and nephews are a few doors away. (DNC/WRL.)

ST. ALBERTUS COMMUNICANTS, 1904. Here is the St. Albertus Church first communion class. Bernard Poblock (Poblocki) is in the second row from the back, far right. Rev. Francis Mueller is on the far left. (AMW.)

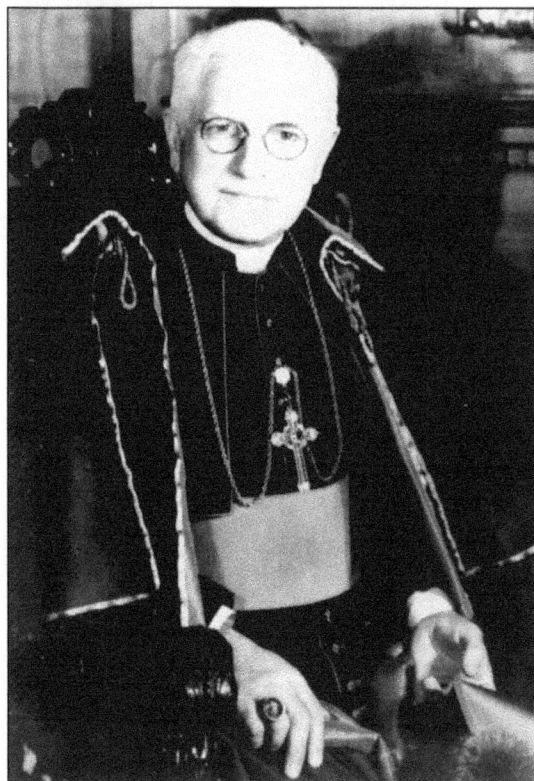

MSGR. JOSEPH CASIMIR PLAGENS (1880–1943). Monsignor Plagens was a graduate of the University of Detroit. He became the pastor of Sweetest Heart of Mary in 1919. He built a permanent convent for the Sisters of St. Joseph, who staffed the school from 1894 until its closure in the 1960s. In 1923, he became the first monsignor of Polish ancestry in Detroit. He became the bishop of Marquette in 1936 and, later, the bishop of Grand Rapids, where he died on March 31, 1943. (AFSLM.)

Ks. Pawel Gutowski (1845–1918).
Born in Brzezno, Poland, Gutowski went
to seminary in Pelplin, Poland, and
was the founding pastor of St. Casimir
Parish in 1882 and remained the pastor
for 35 years. On October 26, 1907, there
was a double silver jubilee—the parish
celebrated its natal day and Gutowski his
25th anniversary of pastorate. (FEW.)

Alice's Classmates, 1903. Shown here is the classroom of "Alice" Leocadia (Glowny) Poblock
(1896–1929), seen in the second row at the far right. The name of the school is not known, but
notice the Polish writing on the blackboard at left. The calligraphy looks like an exercise for the
beautiful cursive handwriting style known as the Palmer method that was popular in the second
two decades of the 20th century. (AMW.)

RODZINA
St. Mieczkowskiego i M. z Szyn
Ślubow.
dnia
20 g

Stanisław 7 Maja '55 Hantzwelde

Marcyan

Jan 13go Maja '80 r. Szonowo

Franciszek 12go Grudnia '85 Grutta

Agnieszka 20go Sierp.'91. Detroit, Mich.

Klara 23go Grudnia. 94. Detroit, Mich.

Gertru

"RODZNIA S. E. MIECZKOWSKI I
M. Z. SZYNKOWISKA" AROUND
1916. The family photographs of
Stanislaw Mieczkowski and his
wife, Marcyanna Szynkowiska, is a
treasure, not only for the charming
formal portraits but also for the family
history contained in the captions.
The family's migration can be traced
by the names of the villages of birth.
Stanislaw was born in Hantzwelde;
Marcyanna and daughter Marya
were born in Lasin; Jan was born in
Szonowo; Franciszek and Antoni were
born in Grutta; and the youngest
daughters, Agnieszka, Gertruda, and
Klara, were born in Detroit. (KAM.)

TEAMSTER PRUSS OFF DUTY AROUND 1911. William Pruss (1893–1955) is seen here with one of his horses, cooling his heels on a warm day. William was the son of Walenty Pruss and Franziska Zolkowski of Laskawnica, Schubin, Posen. He married Martha Chmielewski on October 14, 1913. They had lived across the street from each other on Medbury in Detroit from the time they were born. They were the parents of Chester William Pruss and Genevieve (Pruss) Dunneback. (GPD.)

ZYNDA'S BALTIC DIP, 1912. Widower John Zynda took a trip back to Poland and found a new wife, Anna Sanger. Pictured here is the brewer bathing in the Baltic with wife Anna and her niece and nephews. (FZ.)

TEAMSTER PRUSS. William Pruss is seen here with his team of horses and delivery wagon. Pruss was rarely seen without his cigar. Many Poles made their living as teamsters who owned wagons. Today's International Brotherhood of Teamsters has horses on its logo as a tribute to its earliest members. (GPD.)

BY THE WAY. A good chat with the neighbors was usually conducted in Polish. Many second-generation children remember these scenes when the adults would converse believing the children did not know a word of the language. Soon the youngsters were developing a vocabulary—just to know the adults' secrets. (DNC/WRL.)

GUARDIAN ANGELS. The sisters arrived to set up schools but found they needed to offer support to the immigrant families. They established orphanages for girls and boys and a convent to train new nuns. The girls' orphanage was known as Guardian Angels. An 1889 newspaper article stated, "Few people know the real helpfulness of this Polish order nor guess the extent to which the institution is extending aid to orphans and old people." (FEW.)

CHILDREN OF THE PREUSS FURNITURE COMPANY FAMILY. Frank Preuss was involved in Detroit's thriving cigar business before he owned Preuss Furniture. The children of Frank and Frances (née Rochowiak) are, from left to right, Wanda, Bruno, baby Arthur, Edward, Clara, and Edna (in front). Antoinette Glowny, mother of Alice Glowny Poblock, and her sister Frances Preuss were the daughters of Magdalene and Matthew Rochowiak. The daughters lived in adjacent homes at 274 and 270 Illinois Street in Detroit. (AMW.)

SWEET SHOP, 1914. Rose Merique-Urbin and her youngest son, George, stand in front of their family business, the Standard Confectionery, located on Gratiot directly across from St. Joseph German Catholic Church. Rose's husband opened the store in 1914, and it remained in this location until 1920. Note the sign that advertises 5¢ Jersey creams. (KAM.)

ZDZIEBKO BOYS, C. 1886. Shown here are the sons of Tomasz and Agata Zdziebko. Henry was born in 1873, John in 1877, and Frank in 1879. They came to the United States from Zarzecze, Jaslo, Galicia, in 1879. The photograph was taken in Detroit at the Watson Studio, located at 146 and 148 Woodward Avenue. (FEW.)

HEDWIG "HATTIE" ZIEMBOWICZ AROUND 1914. Hattie's studio photograph is the type new parents would be proud to send back to family members in Poland. Hattie was the daughter of Walter Ziembowicz and Alexandra Ziembowicz (née Gutowski). Her younger siblings were Frank, Leo, and Irene. (DS.)

RODZINA ZALEWSKI AROUND 1925. Stanley Zalewski is shown here on a visit to his parents and family in Brudzen, Poland. Stanley Zalewski (far left) immigrated to the United States with members of his family in the early 20th century. He first worked in the Pennsylvania coal mines. By 1920, he had moved to the Detroit area, seeking employment in automobile plants. Stanley married and had three children. (AMW.)

BORKOWSKI-POBLOCKI FAMILY IN GARCZYN, POLAND, C. 1915. Many Detroit albums include photographs of family members still in Poland. The head of the family was an admiral in the German Navy. August Borkowski (brother of Julianna Borkowski Poblocki) is pictured here with his wife, Agatha Borkowski (née Poblocki). Their children are, from left to right, a nun, a dentist, Sylvester—a lawyer and judge, Sylvester's son, and a teacher. John Poblocki married Julianna Borkowski. Julianna's brother August married John Poblocki's sister, Agatha. (AMW.)

THE SAJEWICZ FAMILY IN POLAND, C. 1911. Franciszek Sajewicz and Magdalena Sajewicz (née Ferkaluk) are shown here with their daughter Rozalia (born in 1895). They lived in Gwozdziec, Kolomyja, Kulakowice, and Galicia. These are the parents of Antoni and Michael Sajewicz of Detroit. They were killed on their farm by Hungarian mercenaries employed by the Russians shortly before their children were to bring them to the United States. (AMW.)

ALEXANDER ZYNDA. John Zynda's brother Alexander stayed in Poland, but the family kept close ties. John remembered his Polish family and community in his will. He left his brothers Frank's and Alexander's children $2,000 and bequeathed money to his Ruchniewicz cousins. He also remembered the welfare department of the city of Kosciezyna and the Polish Sisters of Kosciezyna. (FZ.)

OLSCHEFSKY'S SALOON. In a 1903 article, the *Detroit News* reported that "Reverend Gutowski stated, 'Drinking places should be reduced. In the parish, there were 100 saloons that did as they pleased. Sundays the young men congregated in these places as long as they were warm and comfortable and could get enough to drink. The dance hall was also a great evil. Located over saloons, young men and woman go to the bad on account of their dance hall association.'" (FZ.)

LaBudie Family Portrait. Pictured here is the family of Frank LaBudie, born October 17, 1855, in Kamien, Wejherowo, Gdansk, Poland, and Barbara Burkowski, born in Poznan province. Their son Louis J. LaBudie, born in Detroit on April 16, 1894, was the chief investigator for the prosecutor's office and helped bring the rum-running Purple Gang to justice during Prohibition. (KLS.)

KOLPACKI KOFFEE KLATCH. The married sisters reunite. Included in the group are Helen Laske, Rose Voight, Theresa Pegler, Hanna Grail, Minnie, and mother Anna. (JV.)

ANNA KOLPACKI'S GIRLS. By 1920, Anna and husband Jacob Kolpaki were living on Twenty-third Street, and newlyweds John Wojtkowiak and daughter Rose were living with them. Next door was son John, his wife Francis, and children Margaret, Edward, Leonard, and Harry. (JV.)

Two

BUILDING THE FAMILY
COURTING AND MARRIAGE

ANNA ZYNDA WEDS, 1920S. The wedding photograph of Anna Zynda and Edmund Grocholski took place at the Bellevue Avenue home of her father, brewmaster John Zynda. The grand home was draped in patriotic bunting. The house included a chapel where mass was offered by visiting priests. (FZ.)

GENEVIEVE TUCHEWICZ, 1901–1994. This photograph was taken at the Fios Studio at 61 Monroe Street in Detroit prior to her marriage to Max Ponka in November 1923 at St. Hyacinth in Detroit. Her parents, Antonina Hartka and Jan Tuchewicz, were married in the village of Pokrzydowo, Torun, which is presently in Kujawsko-Pomorskie. (VWK.)

COVER GIRL. Leocadia Poblock Bojarski's photograph was used on the cover of a cigar box. She worked in a cigar factory on the east side of Detroit. Tobacco production was one of the largest industries in Detroit at the turn of the 20th century. She was born in Garczyn, in the Kaszuby region near Gdansk. She immigrated to the United States with her family in September 1893. (AMW.)

RECZEK SISTERS. While little is know about this photograph of Mary and Katherine from the Reczek family, their style and grace are timeless. The photograph was taken in a Detroit studio, sent to Poland, and returned to the Detroiters by Polish relatives a century later. Portraits like this send descendants scrambling to find the jewelry worn in the photograph. In this case, there is a brooch and a woman's watch. Mary wed Paul Wojdyla, and Katherine married Andrew Sitek. (CF.)

MARTHA'S VIGNETTE, 1911. Martha Pruss (née Chmielewski), 1893–1970, wife of William Pruss, is pictured here. She was the daughter of Jan Chmielewski and Anna Chmielewski (née Kloska) of Poland. She was also the mother of Chester William Pruss and Genevieve Marie Dunneback (née Pruss). (GPD.)

LERCH AND LEMANSKA WEDDING. Charles Lerch/Lark (1852–1927) and his wife Angela Lemanska (1852–1881) are shown here on their wedding day, June 25, 1876, at St. Albertus Church. Both the Lerch/Lark and Lemanski families were pioneer Polish settlers in Detroit. (KAM.)

VICTORIA DRZEWIECKA, C. 1915.
Victoria was the niece of the prominent
brewer Thomas Zoltowski. She was
born in 1895, so it is possible she
witnessed the lavish 1899 wedding of
her cousin Anna Zoltowska to Dr. S. J.
Lachajewski, chronicled in the *Detroit
News.* "A chorus of Ahs began as the
bridesmaids entered, and they sounded
just the same in Polish as in English.
Anna wore a white duchess satin,
trimmed in real lace, a long tulle veil
and bridal roses completed the picture
in white." (DBO.)

TRUMPETERS, C. 1910. Pictured here are
unknown fellows from the photo postcard
album of Anthony and Cecilia Przytulski.
The men may have worked with Tony at the
cigar factory and were certainly friends he
accompanied on his guitar. (FEW.)

INGÉNUE. This is also an unidentified photo postcard from Anthony and Cecilia Przytulski's collection. The young woman is wearing a soft-printed cotton dress, and the photographer posed her in profile. Perhaps it is a photograph for her beau? (FEW.)

LILLIAN'S ENGAGEMENT. Their late mother's sister, who was always referred to as Aunt Pisarek, guided Lillian, along with the other Ewald children. Lillian is photographed here wearing a gold bracelet. She married Walter Lesinski on June 23, 1920. Stella Pisarek advised the young couples that it was chic to receive an engagement bracelet instead of a ring. When her nephew Anthony presented a bracelet to Cecilia, she joked it was handcuffs. (FEW.)

POLA NEGRI?. Anna Ewald, pictured around 1910, may have had Polish actress Pola Negri in mind when she shadowed her eyes for this engagement photograph. A few years younger than Pola, Anna was born in 1901. Negri (Barbara Apollonia Chalipec) was a favorite with Poles and at one time was engaged to Rudolph Valentino and, later, Charlie Chaplin. (FEW.)

BETROTHED, C. 1910. Here is an engagement photograph of Bertha Szeperanski from the collection of Cecilia Przytulski. Bertha married Joseph Kopczynski and had a daughter, Gertrude, and sons Joseph, Robert, and Harry. In 1930, they lived at 5363 Thirty-second Street. (FEW.)

BELLE ISLE GENT, C. 1910. Anthony Przytulski poses in his Sunday best, including a Detroit-made cigar and his beer stein. This Sunday he was accompanied by his fiancée, Cecilia Wojtkowiak, her sister Katherine and her fiancée, Richard Topolewski, and their brothers' families John and Rose, Joe and Anna Wojtkowiak. (FEW.)

BELLE ISLE BOATING, C. 1910. Rose Voight is given a push by her husband Joe. Canoes were rented for a trip on the 2.2 miles of canals and interconnected lakes. While the exact date is unknown, the American flag on the bow and the crowds on the beach and on the Central Avenue Bridge suggest the Fourth of July. (FEW.)

PUT-IN-BAY, C. 1913. William and Martha are shown here at Put-in-Bay Island Park, Ohio. William and Martha Pruss posed for a souvenir photograph on a possible church outing. Notice her ribbon pin. Advertisements for the park encouraged visitors to take the steamer and enjoy "Entertainment Galore Afloat and Ashore." The steamer left Detroit at 10:00 a.m. and returned at 10:45 p.m. (GPD.)

COURTING, 1910. Cecilia wears a tulle hat as she jokes with Anthony while picnicking at Belle Isle. Cecilia's mother considered Anthony a good boyfriend since he always left the house at a reasonable time. It was actually the whistle of a buddy that signaled it was time to leave and meet at the beer garden. Cecilia's hat is similar to the one featured on the September 1910 cover of the *McCall's* magazine. (FEW.)

Agata Zdziebko Weds, November 28, 1899. Frank Wendt from Mestin, Mühlbanz, Dirschau, Westpreußen, married Agata Zdziebko from Zarzecze, Dembowiec, Jaslo, Galicia. This would have been unusual in Poland since their villages were 80 kilometers apart. Distanced from their home villages, Frank and Agata found that their origins in Poland were not as important, and it was their shared religion, customs, and culture that made them compatible. Agata died in 1908 from typhoid fever, a common disease at the time, and left behind five children. (FEW.)

MARY ZDZIEBKO WEDS, OCTOBER 20, 1908. After the death of Agata, Frank followed a Polish custom and married his sister-in-law Mary. Not fond of the arrangement, she is said to have prayed for the sidewalk to open and take her as they approached the church. Both bride and groom wear their wedding bands on the right hand, a European tradition. (FEW.)

FIRST OF 60 YEARS, OCTOBER 16, 1912. Anthony Przytulski and Cecilia Wojtkowiak were wed at St. Casimir Parish. This photograph was taken on their wedding day at the F. Ziawinski studio located at 1652 Michigan Avenue. Cecilia (born in 1890) and Anthony (born in 1890) became parents of three boys and six girls. They celebrated their 50th and 60th wedding anniversaries surrounded by family. Their marriage lasted for 64 years until Anthony's death in 1976 and Cecilia a few months later in 1977. As of 2005, they have five succeeding generations and 98 descendants. (FEW.)

MARY ADAMSKA WOJTKOWIAK HENNING. Mary left Swiatniki, Rogalinek, Schrimm, Posen, in 1888 to join her husband Peter Wojtkowiak, in Calumet, Michigan. Nine years later, she was a widow with seven children. She is shown here with her second husband, Charles Henning. The marriage allowed her to bring her children home from the orphanage. (FEW.)

BALLERINAS? AUGUST 8, 1916. Katherine Wojtkowiak (1893–1987), bride of Richard Topolewski (1892–1960), poses with her new sisters-in-law, Celia, Lottie, and Kate. The marriage took place at St. Casimir Parish. The photograph was taken by Joseph Sowinski, a photographer from Poland who ran a studio and photograph school and lived in Detroit for 66 years. (FEW.)

45

LARK AND MERIQUE WEDDING, JUNE 8, 1926. Walter Gustave Merique and Rosalia Helen Lark wed. The photograph was taken at the Smart Set Studio. Walter Phillips was best man, and Marie Derio Nigro was the maid of honor. Typical of many Polish weddings, the celebration lasted five days. (KAM.)

CYROWSKI WEDS LARK. On August 19, 1903, A. Edward Lark and Josephine Theresa Cyrowski married. This photograph was taken by Joseph Sowinski. The wedding united two of the most influential Polish families in Detroit. The couple had two daughters. (KAM.)

LOST AND FOUND, C. 1912. This photograph was thought to be a family wedding but was unidentified for 50 years. It was not until Jepko cousins in Detroit and Chicago linked up on the Internet that a portrait photograph with all the family members' names was found. The Zdziebko wedding was identified as the marriage of Joseph Zdziebko (Japko) and Stella C. Rybicki, with sisters Mary and Anna and brother Frank in attendance. (FEW.)

FRANK CHMIELEWSKI (1897–1974).
Pictured here in Detroit, Frank was
the son of Jan Chmielewski and Anna
Chmielewski (née Kloska) of Poland.
He was the brother of Martha Pruss
(née Chmielewski) and uncle to Chester
William Pruss and Genevieve Marie
Dunneback (née Pruss). (GPD.)

HELEN OWIESNY, 1923. Helen
(1908–1964) was a first-generation Pole,
born in Detroit to Stephen Owiesny
and Marianna Drzewiecka. This
picture of Helen at age 23 was taken
at the wedding of her sister Anna.
She was the grandniece of Detroit's
high-profile Thomas Zoltowski, "the
King of the Poles." At the time of
this picture, she lived in Detroit
on East Warren Avenue. (DBO.)

SITEK AND LUDWIG NUPTIALS, 1927.
Helen Sitek wed Louis Ludwig on
Feburary 23, 1927. Under her beautiful
lace veil, Helen has her hair finished
in pin curls in the latest fashion. Louis
and Helen had one daughter. (CF.)

OUR LADY QUEEN OF HEAVEN. The church began in a storefront on Van Dyke at Bliss Street.
Rev. Albert Mrowka, the pastor, shown here celebrating mass, built a two-story school, with
the church on the first floor. The wedding is of Sgt. Raymond Cieszynski to Mary Sajewicz,
December 26, 1942. (AMW.)

SW. KUNEGUNDY. Unidentified newlyweds are greeted with a shower of rice as they leave the St. Cunegunda Church. The style of gown suggests a 1940s wedding. (PTF.)

BREAD AND SALT. This image shows a Polish custom still practiced in Poland and continued in Detroit. According to Old Polish tradition, the saying goes: We greet you with bread and salt, so that your home might always enjoy abundance. (*Staropolskim zwyczajem witamy Was chlebem i sola, aby w Waszym domu zawsze goscil dostatek.*) (PTF.)

ITALIANO, C. 1939. The engagement of Genevieve Przytulska and Bruno Benedetti caused a stir since he was not Polish. But the path to marrying an Italian had been paved by Genevieve's older sister Virginia, who married Albert Dominic DiNatale on June 1, 1931. (FEW.)

WEDDING SERENADE, MAY 7, 1946. Typical of Polish weddings, Cecilia Gasiorek leaves home with her wedding party on the way to St. John Cantius to wed Joseph Suchyta. Pan Drapczyk and his son Paulie play saxophone and accordion to announce the nuptials to the neighborhood. This was a weekday wedding, Tuesday, May 7. (TW.)

PRZYTULSKA AND WENDT WEDDING, NOVEMBER 18, 1942. This is a photograph of Frank J. Wendt and Elizabeth C. Przytulska's wedding at Assumption BVM Church. Her uncle Richard Topolewski's 1941 Cadillac seems to be the photographer's focus. This is a six-passenger sedan and a fine car for a self-made man in the Motor City. Topolewski, pictured at the left of the car, owned Top Screw and Nut, a factory that supplied automobile companies and the military. Elizabeth was his bookkeeper. (FEW.)

Three

FIRST GENERATION
JOBS, BUSINESSES,
AND MILITARY DUTY

ZYNDA WAGON. This early delivery wagon bears the name of John Zynda's White Eagle Brewery. The workers hold bottles and brew, and additional imbibers are at the door of the brewery. It seems the horse had to be bribed to hold his position. A hand holding something tasty can be seen at the far right. (FZ.)

POLISH DAILY RECORD. The *Polish Daily Record* was located at 1817–1819 Forest Street from 1913 to 1933. The staff of the *Polish Daily Record* and *Polish Sunday Record* is shown here around 1925. Jan Szaroleta is third from the left. Jan's son John states, "Jan worked for the Polish newspaper during the 1920s and became the managing editor. He had worked for a publisher in Stevens Point, Wisconsin, in late 1918–1919." Leopold Koscinski organized Polonia Publishing Company, which published the *Polish Daily Record*. He was also the president. (JS.)

POLISH SUNDAY RECORD. John Kaminski, born in West Prussia, came to Detroit as a child in 1884. He attended the Detroit College of Law and became a prominent Detroit attorney. Kaminski was one of the organizers of the *Polish Daily Record*. He may be the gent on the left in each photograph. Joseph Gardulski, an attorney, served as an editor for the paper. Born in Radomysl, Poland, he attended law school in Krakow and Detroit. (JS.)

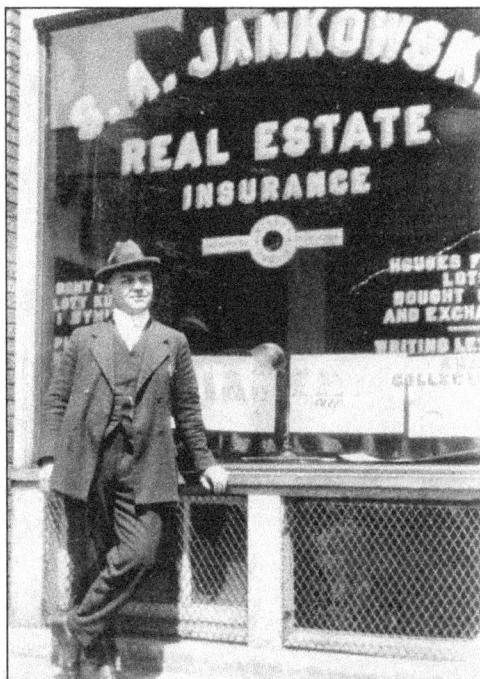

JANKOWSKI REAL ESTATE. Between 1919 and 1926, this pictured storefront at 919 (present-day address 4713) Chene (between Forest and Hancock) served as an insurance and realty office for Stanley A. Jankowski. Jankowski was also the owner of the North End Recreation Bowling Alleys. (RCJ.)

THE POLONIA BAKING COMPANY, 1925. The baking company was located at the corner of Thirtieth and Herbert Streets on Detroit's west side. Two recent immigrants from Poland, Vincent Lisowski and Sophia Lisowski (née Mizera), bought the business in 1917 after saving $5,000 to purchase it. They had seven delivery vans delivering baked goods all over Detroit, Delray, and Hamtramck. During the Great Depression, pastries sold for 25¢ per dozen fresh and 10¢ per dozen for day-old. Vincent Lisowski and his three children, Lucy, Ziggie, and Helen, are accompanied by some neighborhood children. (JLS.)

OSTROWSKA AND WOJTKOWIAK, SEPTEMBER 1, 1919. Joseph F. Voight (1892–1932), whose surname changed from Wojtkowiak, and Anna M. Ostrowska (1894–1972) married at St. Casimir Church. He wore his army uniform for the wedding portrait. They had two sons, Richard and Arthur. Joseph made it back safe from World War I only to be beaten to death by thugs at a White Castle while defending a waitress in 1932. (FEW.)

JOHN VOIGHT WED ROSE KOLPACKI. Brothers John and Joseph both were in the U.S. Army during World War I. Like many soldiers, John Wojtkowiak wed Rose Kolpacki in his military uniform. They married April 10, 1918. Family members officially changed their surname to Voight in the 1930s. John and Rose had six children, including Norbert, who was killed in action during World War II at Okinawa. John visited the grave each year when his World War II Polar Bears veterans held memorial services at White Chapel Cemetery in Troy. (FEW.)

BELLE ISLE WELCOME, JULY 4, 1919. Detroiters welcome home the 339th Infantry, the "Polar Bears," at a Belle Isle rally. (DNC/WRL.)

POLAR BEAR 25TH REUNION, 1944. The Polar Bear Association was devoted to all veterans of the North Russian expeditionary forces. The organization was active at least until 1983, when 22 surviving members of the association held a luncheon meeting in Detroit. (JV.)

HALLER'S ARMY, C. 1918. Kneeling third from left is Hipolit Wagner. Born in Idalin, Lublin Province, Poland, in 1894, he immigrated to the United States in 1913. He was a member of the Polish Falcons, where he received paramilitary training. He was inducted into the Polish Army in France under General Haller in 1918. He was active with the Polish Legion of America veterans' group and other organizations. (AMW.)

HALLER'S II, C. 1919. Many Poles from Detroit volunteered at the request of Ignacy Paderewski. They fought in the campaigns against the Germans in France in 1918 and against the Soviets in Poland in 1919–1921. The Polish Army picture came from the Sitek/Zawacki album. (CF.)

LOUIS AT WORK. Louis Mormol of Hammond worked at the local gas station and posed with the owner, Sam. Typical of the time is the station's tiled roof. (BMW.)

CADILLAC PUBLISHING, 1935. Bernard Poblock (Poblocki), printer, is shown here (rear right) with colleagues. In 1893, Poblock emigrated as a child with his mother, Julianna, from Garczyn, Koscierzyna, Kaszuby. In addition to his career as a printer, he owned a haberdashery and billiards parlor on Chene Street. He was one of the founders of the Outer-Van Dyke Home Owners Association, as well as printing and editing their newsletter, *"Hi" Neighbor.* (AMW.)

S. UPINA

S. SKONIECZNA

A. NOWAK

J. WAIS

K. SITEK

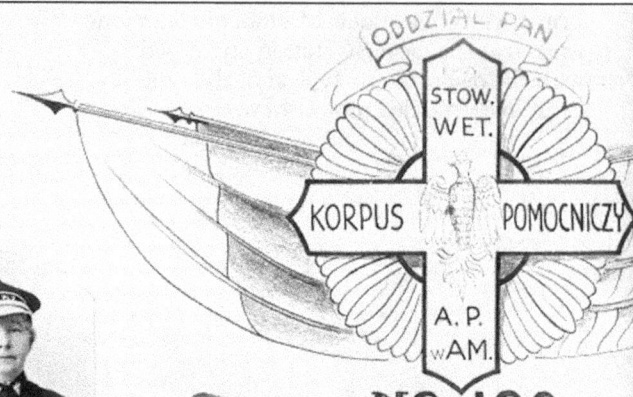

STOW. WET. KORPUS POMOCNICZY A. P. w AM.

NO. 109.
DETROIT, MICH.

M. HARANCZAK
1-SZA VICE-PREZ.

M. STANOWSKA
PREZESKA

S. TROCHIM

M. ROSINSKA

S. SADOWSKA

M. MOSKWA
SEKR. PROTOK

C. SKIERKOWSKA
KASJERKA

F. WASIELEWSKA

M. SPLEET

J. KOWALSKA

H. PRICE

P. ZAJDEL
MARSZAŁ.

J. LEŚNIEWSKA

A. GINNIS

JACKOWSKA

A. SITEK

S. ORBIK

K. JANISZEWSKA

S. BOIKE

R. RUTKOWSKA

M. ZABŁOCKA

M. PIECUCH

J. GRZYMAŁA

E. LEWANDOWSKA

W. BUCZYNSKA

SWAP No. 109. Persons who fought in Polish units in the First World War, the 1918–1921 war, and the Second World War who lived outside Poland were often members of the *Stowarzyszenie Weteranow Armii Polskiej* (SWAP) or, in English, the Polish Army Veterans Association. Pictured here is Mary Sitek Stanowski who was born in 1905 to Albert Sitek and Katherine Reczek. She married Joseph Stanowski. Her sister Anna and mother Katherine were also involved with the benevolent society.

H. Wagner Grocery, 1939. From left to right are a customer and the Wagner family, including Hipolit (1894–1960), Helen (1904–1978), Stan, Adele, Lorraine, and Arthur. The customer is pointing to a Farm Crest cakes display. The photograph was a gift from the Farm Crest distributor. In 1945, the Wagner family moved to 19430 Packard in northeast Detroit and remained there until 1978. (AMW.)

Corner Store, 1941. Taking a short break from working in their confectionery store, the Kurzyniec family (Stasia, Dot, the mother, and Martha), pose for a picture on Pulaski Street in Delray. The building on the right is the original St. John Cantius Church, which became a hall when the new church was constructed in 1922. The movie poster advertises *Golden Hoofs* at the Grande Theater. Merchandise in the window includes a High Flyer paper kite, Vernor's ginger ale, and Mail Pouch tobacco for smokers who rolled their own cigarettes. (CGS.)

JOHN ZYNDA AND SONS, LATE 1920S OR EARLY 1930S. During Prohibition, the Zyndas' brewery theoretically stopped beer production and sold cereal and carbonated beverages, including chocolate soda. The decorated truck is adorned with a tray with the likeness of John Zynda himself. (FZ.)

SUCHYTA'S BAKERY. Stores on wheels were common in Detroit neighborhoods. Vegetables and baked goods, as well as milk and dairy products were delivered door to door. Here Frank Suchyta's truck (bakery located on Martin near Michigan Avenue) advertises fancy pies, bread, and cakes. (CGS.)

FATHER AND SON, 1942. Joseph Suchyta and his father, Joseph Sr., pose on Copland Street for a light-hearted photograph during World War II. Father Joseph wears his son's dress military visor cap while Joseph Jr. is wearing a garrison cap and khakis. (CGS.)

STELLA THE RIVETER, 1939. Stella "Stacia" Mormol tackles machine No. 8, which was twice her size, at Fitzsimmons Manufacturing Company. Stacia, in gillie shoes and a hair bow, was photographed on March 2, 1939. (BMW.)

TYE AND TYE, C. 1942. Joseph and father Jan (John) Tyc are pictured here. Jan was born on June 21, 1891, in Czerwienski Stare, parish of Baranowo. He came to America in 1910. Joseph was born on May 11, 1918, in St. Louis, Missouri. He changed his name from Tyc to Tye in 1943. Jan married Rozialia Krajewska (1894–1946) on August 26, 1913, at St. Casimir Church, in St. Louis. Jan died in Detroit on July 13, 1960. Jan and Rozialia were parents to seven children. (JT.)

WEEKEND WEDDING, NOVEMBER 28, 1942. The Dyda's Delray grocery store located at 625 Leigh Street was a family affair and had to be staffed by Sophia, even on the day her sister Cecilia was standing up in a wedding. Cecilia was in the wedding party for Joseph and Stephanie Staron. Many weddings, including Cecilia's, actually took place on weekdays during World War II. (CGS.)

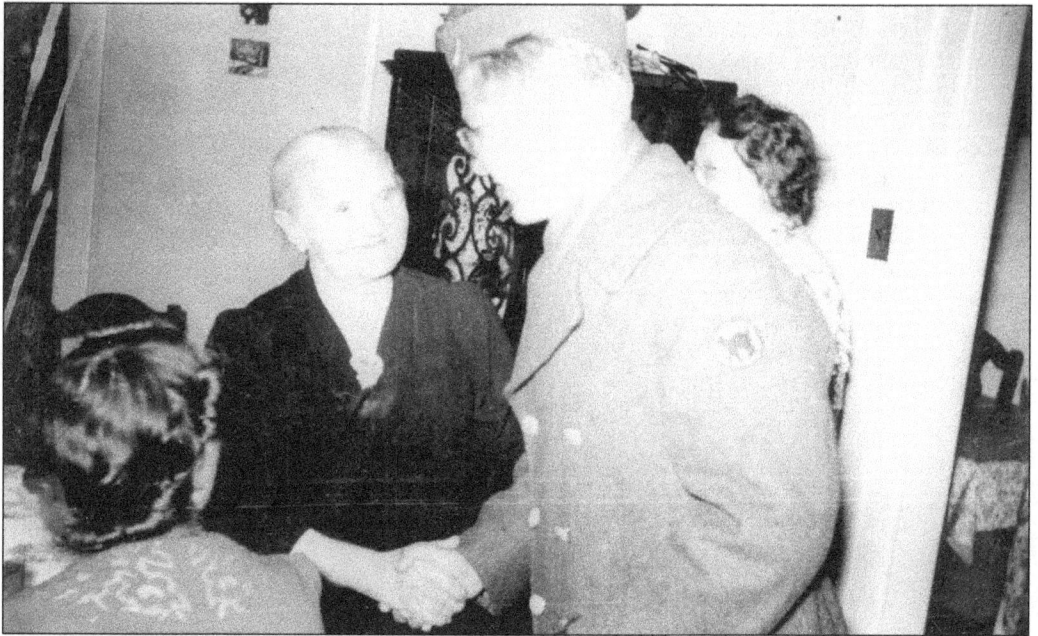

MARY'S SOLDIERS. Mary Henning saw three sons off to World War I. John and Joseph Wojtkowiak served in the U.S. Army and Peter in the Navy. She also saw her grandsons serve. Pfc. Norbert J. Voight, U.S. Army, was killed in action in Okinawa, and Paul F. Pokryfky was severely wounded at Cherbourg, France, and received the Purple Heart. Brothers Raymond, Patrick, James (pictured here), and Robert Topolewski all served and returned from their tour of duty, as did their cousin Anthony Przytulski Jr., who received two Bronze Stars. (FEW.)

HEADLINES. Soldiers followed the headlines after they returned home. Here Patrick Topolewski reads the headline of the *Detroit News*, "Red Arrow Division Cited." (PTF.)

ANTHONY PRZYTULSKI JR. Anthony was in battles and campaigns in Rhineland and Central Europe. His decorations and citations include the American Theater ribbon, European Theater ribbon with two Bronze Stars, World War II victory ribbon, and a Bronze Star received during the Rhineland campaign. (FEW.)

PATRICK J. TOPOLEWSKI (1919–2000). Patrick joined three of his brothers in the service. His parents, Richard and Katherine, sent their four oldest children off to war: Raymond (1917), Patrick (1919), James (1921), and Robert (1923). All four returned home, where their younger brothers, Gerry and Marvin, and sister, Lorraine, waited. (PTF.)

SAILOR BARNEY BLASS. Barney was born in 1916 and Irene in 1918. They will observe 70 years of marriage in 2006. Some will remember when the Blass were Blasziewicz. Barney served in the navy during World War II and worked all his life in the automobile industry at Vickers and GM as a tradesman. He was from the west side around St. Francis of Assisi. They are one of the longest-married couples in Dearborn.

THEO. Theodore Stankiewicz (Stanton), 1916–1990, is seen here in the pith helmet. He served in the Pacific theater with the U.S. Army during World War II. The pith helmet was made of cork and was strong and protective while at the same time lightweight and comfortable. The soldier could immerse the hat in water, keeping him cool during in the Pacific theater. (VWK.)

MANHATTAN PROJECT. T4 Walter Sajewicz (1916–1962) served in the U.S. Army from 1945 to 1946 as an engineering aide in the atom bomb (Manhattan) project (see arm insignia). Educated at St. Francis Home for Boys, Burroughs Intermediate, and Wilbur Wright Vocational High School, Sajewicz lived with his wife, Jane, and daughters, Magdalene and Carol, in the Outer Drive–Van Dyke area. His father, Antoni Sajewicz, immigrated from Koscierzyna, Kolomyja, Galicia, Poland/Ukraine. (AWM.)

VALENTINE WARUNEK, 1926–1998. Valentine Warunek completed a course to be an aerial gunner at Harlingen, Texas, in 1944 and received a medal for being able to use a pistol. He sailed home in February 1947, on the *Zebulon B. Vance*. Warunek's war photographs supplied the information. (VWK.)

69

STACHURSKA AND PRZYTULSKI, C. 1943.
Lottie and Tony are pictured here at
Christmastime at Tony's parents home on
Twenty-eighth Street. Tony had his attorney
brother-in-law Frank Wendt pull a few
strings at city hall so he and Lottie could get
married on his April leave. Leocadia Victoria
Stahurska and Anthony J. Przytulski Jr. were
wed April 15, 1944. Their marriage was
fruitful. They had five sons and celebrated
their 50th anniversary in 1994. (FEW.)

SGT. RAYMOND AND MARY CIESZYNSKI, DECEMBER 26, 1942. The marriage brought together
two east-side neighborhood families, the Cieszynski and the Sajewicz. Raymond extended his leave
a few days in order to attend his already planned wedding. When he rejoined his unit, the officers
congratulated him and took away his stripes and put him in the brig for a few days for being AWOL.
He earned a Purple Heart for his part in the invasion of Sicily. (AMW.)

Four

GROWING UP
SACRAMENTS, PARISHES, AND SCHOOLS

ST. CASIMIR SCHOOL, C. 1898. Room five must have been a rambunctious place. One hundred years after the photograph was taken, the cheeky boys in knickers seem to bounce off the page. Antoni Przytulski (the back row, fifth from the right) arrived in Detroit in 1896 from Kuczbork-Osada, Zuromin, Russian Poland. Like many of his generation, his schooling was cut short. St. Casimir School, located at 3361 Twenty-third Street, opened in 1883 and closed on June 18, 2005. (FEW.)

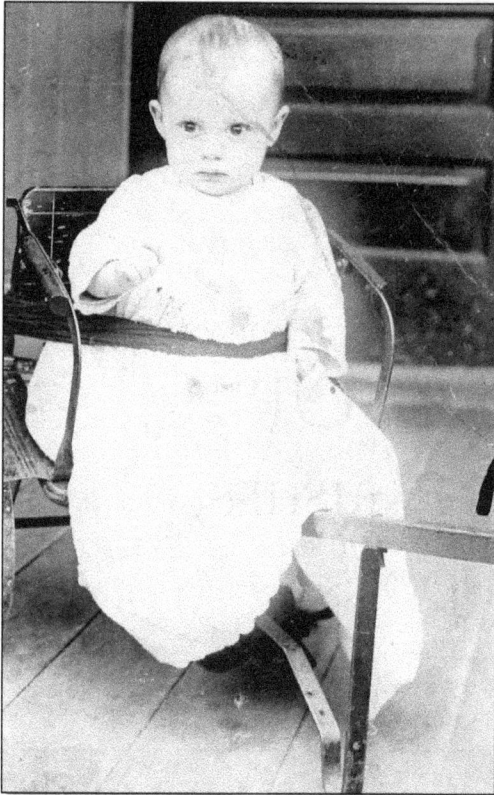

CHESTER WILLIAM PRUSS (1914–1966), AROUND 1915. Even before car seats, Chester's mom knew how to keep him safe on the porch. Chester was the son of William Pruss and Martha Pruss (née Chmielewski) and grandson of Walenty Pruss and Franziska Pruss (née Zolkowski). Chester grew up on the east side of Detroit and attended Cass Tech and Wilbur Wright High Schools. He was an accountant for the old Packard Motor Car Company in Detroit for 23 years until they went out of business. (GPD.)

ANNE'S PORCELAIN DOLL, 1917. Anne and Martha Trepczynski pose with Anne's treasured doll. Years after this photograph was taken, Anne would long for the doll. It was forgotten in a move. When the family went back to claim the doll, the new owners had not seen it. (LRD.)

CHRISTMAS BIKE, 1925. Tony proudly rides the bike he received for Christmas. Since times were tough with nine children in the family, his mother, Cecilia, wondered where she could find enough money for his gift. She arranged with a friend to work at Carhartt's clothing for a few weeks to earn enough for the children's Christmas presents. Tony's older sister Leona Przytulska looks on. (FEW.)

TRAVELING PHOTOGRAPHER, C. 1914. Hattie Ziembowicz (Samull) poses on a donkey in a photograph taken by a traveling photographer in Detroit's east-side Polish neighborhood around St. Albertus. Hattie was about one year old. Every family album has a photograph of a child on a pony or a donkey. It was a Detroit neighborhood tradition for three generations. Here Hattie sits sidesaddle, a pretty good job for such a small girl. (DS.)

SCHEWE/SZEWA, 1908. The Schewe family sits for a formal photograph. From left to right are Frances, mother Julianna, Pauline, John, Theresa, father August, and Leo. Julianna Catherina Schewe (née Wendt) was born December 20, 1871, in Mahlin, Mühlbanz Parish, Westpreußen, and came to the United States aboard the *Oldenburg*. She arrived at the port of Baltimore on April 14, 1892. She wed August J. Schewe in Detroit about 1897. (FEW.)

STUDIO VOIGHTS, 1924. Peter Voight and Hattie Voight (née Blancke) returned to the neighborhood studio near Assumption BVM Church where they had their May 14, 1919, wedding photograph taken. They returned in 1924 with their children Eleanor, Ethel, and Ervin. (FEW.)

BACKYARD PRZYTULSKIS, 1920. Sometimes families posed for casual family portraits. Anthony holds his first son, Bernard, with daughters Betty, Genevieve, and Virginia in almost matching homemade eyelet dresses. Mother Cecilia holds Leona, born on March 10, 1920. (FEW.)

STUDIO WOZNIAKS, 1919. Here is a fine father and son studio portrait from the Wozniak album. Both are wearing hats in the protocol of the day. Father Ignacy Wozniak (1887–1933) holds son Alfred Zigfred Wozniak (1916–1988). After Ignacy died in 1933, Alfred went to work to support the family rather than finish his senior year of high school. (TW.)

CECILIA'S COMMUNION. A child's first communion warranted a studio photograph. Cecilia Wojtkowiak poses with long black hose and button-top shoes. She was living at the Felician Sisters orphanage and learned to sew by making habits for the nuns. She later made clothing for her own family. (FEW.)

GUARDIAN ANGELS' CHAPEL. In 1895, the *Detroit Free Press* reported, "The object and scope of the [Guardian Angels'] was the maintenance of Polish orphans. A happy, well-disciplined company in their merry red frocks, the children played under the supervision of lay sisters under the grapevines. Either the Poles are a particularly hearty race and bear transplanting well, or the little ones had been most carefully watched out for as there were no sick or ailing children to demand sympathy." (AFSLM.)

Virginia and Elizabeth, 1923. Cecilia made clothing for her own family. Her daughters, Elizabeth and Virginia, are pictured in dresses sewn on her treadle machine. Always a practical Pole, she dyed the white dresses peach afterward so the girls could wear them on other occasions. (FEW.)

Tyc Brothers, 1931. Stanley, Walter, and Joseph are shown here in 1931. Stanley and Joseph had just completed eighth grade at Immaculate Conception Grade School. Walter was at his first communion. (JT.)

WALTER SITEK. Walter Sitek was an altar boy at Sweetest Heart of Mary parish. Joe Rudzinski remembered, "We had several different cassocks, i.e., Red and Black. Red for the normal and joyous occasions and Black for lent and funerals. We did have the Caplet but that was only worn on special occasions, i.e., processions etc. We used a white surplice also." (CF.)

ISABELLA SOCIETY AROUND 1910. Martha Pruss (née Chmielewski), left, was a member of the Isabella Society. Believed to be the same Isabella Society named to honor Columbus's sponsor, Queen Isabella of Castile, and the organization advocated educational freedom for women. (GPD.)

GEORGE VOIGHT, ALTAR BOY AT ASSUMPTION BVM, 1923. John Szaroleta remembered, "I loved being the big deal with the incense . . . the more smoke the better . . . and incensing the congregation. There was something unusual about serving the Friday night Novena. It always seemed more relaxed and more like a celebration with God, especially singing Tantum Ergo and O Salutaris. Christmas midnight mass during the war years was packed especially with servicemen on leave and when they turned out the lights except for the manger and sang *Cicha Noc* there was not a dry eye in the house." (FEW.)

MAY PROCESSION. Children from St. John Cantius School in Delray march in May Procession down Pulaski Street to honor the Blessed Mother. The altar boys led the way while the Felician Sisters guided their classes—each preceded by a banner. The festivities ended at the church with a ceremony, benediction, and hymns. (TW.)

BROTHER AND SISTER'S COMMUNION, C. 1926. Here is Frank and Vivian Brzezinski's first holy communion at St. Hyacinth. Vivian was married there. Frank was born about 1916 and Vivian about 1918. Parents were Helen Tuchewicz and Frank Brzezinski. (VWK.)

VALENTINE'S BAPTISM, 1926. Valentine was born on February 22, 1926, in Detroit to Anna and Jozef Warunek. Anna Wojsowicz came from a little village called Budy, and Jozef was born in Hucisko, near Kolbuszowa, province of Rzeszow. Valentine was baptized on February 28, 1926, at St. Stephen's in Detroit and is pictured here with his godparents, Anthony Kasa and Mary Wojas. (VWK.)

HERBIE AND BERNICE, C. 1930.
Herbert (born in 1928) was two years
old when this photograph was taken
with his sister Bernice (born in 1923),
who was about seven years old. The
Stankiewicz family lived on Warren and
later moved to Montlieu according to
the 1920 and 1930 Detroit census. Their
parents were Anna Tuchewicz and
Theodore Stankiewicz. (VWK.)

SAMULLS' ON CHENE. Walking near the
corner of Chene and Superior Streets near
Emil's gas station and the family homestead,
uncle Edward Samull (1905–1951) is holding
the hand of his nephew Don Samull. (DS.)

FRIENDS JENNIE BUTKA AND KATE MUSZYNSKI, C. 1910. This postcard was part of Anthony and Cecilia Przytulski's collection. Bertha Butka and her sister Jennie lived at 413 Lovett with parents John and Eva. Jennie and her sister Frances were garment makers. They may have sewn the lovely light summer dresses. Kate lived next door to the Ostrowski family (page 15). Kate was also a garment worker. Her sister Victoria was a cigar maker. (FEW.)

RECZEK SISTERS. The young women are stunning. We can imagine them planning for days on what they would wear and how they would fashion their hair. They chose to wear their hair in a pompadour with a hidden support underneath, adorned with a fabric flower at the top and a dark bow at the nape of the neck. Earrings and lace caplets with satin bows set with a rhinestone pin are additional accessories. They also are wearing watch chains, and the woman on the right has her watch attached with a fleur-de-lis pin. (CF.)

FRANK WENDT JR., J.D. Wendt was born at Buchanan and Thirtieth Streets in 1904, where his father Frank Wendt Sr. operated a grocery store and tavern for many years. He received his education at Assumption School, Northwestern High, and the University of Detroit. He worked his way through his high school as an iceman and then in a gas station during college. He graduated from the University of Detroit in 1928 with a law degree. His class included Bachor, Bydlowski, Kuenzel, Mandelowski, Odusky, Oleszkowicz, Popp, Repke, Sosnowski, Stefanski, and Zmuda. (FEW.)

ASSUMPTION, BVM, 1918. Pictured here is one of the early graduating classes of Assumption BVM grade school. The school was open from 1911 until 1989. Each year the graduation class grew. In 1928, there were 56 graduates. This group of 10 students includes Frank Wendt (1904–1964), front row, second from left. (FEW.)

RALPH VOIGHT'S CLASSROOM. Here is St. Leo's classroom. Ralph Voight is in second row, middle. All the girls are in their school uniform. (JV.)

FELICIAN ACADEMY, 1929. "It was originally known as the Seminary of the Felician Sisters and was established in 1882 to 'provide instruction for the young in the several branches of learning which qualify them for their position in life.' At first the Seminary was an exclusive convent boarding school. In 1920, the school accepted lay students. In the first fifty years of existence (1882–1932), 1,028 graduates became members of the community and 180 joined the Felician order." —*Seventy Years of Service*, 1949. (AFSLM.)

ST. CASIMIR. The Felician Sisters took charge of the St. Casimir School on June 1, 1883. Once the school was organized, the parish grew rapidly. From the initial enrollment of 182 pupils in 1883, the school expanded to 1,170 pupils in 1923–1924. "In 1921 the segregation of boys and girls was ended. Two outstanding graduates of the school are Joseph C. Plagens D.D. and Congressman John D. Dingell Sr." —*Seventy Years of Service*, 1949.

St. Albertus, c. 1930s. The priest in the middle is a pastor, Fr. Bernard Ciesielski. Joseph (Stachelski) Stack is in the back row. Some of the girls may be from the Guardian Angel Home across the street from the church. "In 1873 the parish school was built in which teachers were employed until 1879 when five Felician Sisters arrived. By 1882 the parish numbered 1,000. A new school was needed and John Lemke and Anthony Ostrowski provided the funding to erect a building at Canfield and St. Aubin." —*Seventy Years of Service*, 1949. (DS.)

ST. ALBERTUS, MAY 28, 1933. The eighth-grade graduation class is pictured. "Rev. Frank Mueller was the pastor of St. Albertus for 19 years (1894–1913). His successor Rev. Joseph F. Herr erected a new modern school building in 1916, when the enrollment reached

"1,300 pupils." —*Seventy Years of Service*, 1949. The school was designed by architect Harry Rill, who also designed St. Stanislaus Church, Our Lady of Mount Carmel Church in Wyandotte, St. Hedwig's Church, and the school building for St. Hyacinth Church. (KAM.)

BERNADINE (BERNIE) AND BERNARD (BARNEY). Bernadine Sitek and Bernard Karaskiewicz met in a dance class where they were both taking lessons. They are standing on the porch at 4738 Riopelle Street, Bernie's grandmother Catherine Sitek's house. They performed for the Polish Falcon Banquet and a GM event. Bernadine remembers auditioning for the Ted Mack Amateur Hour. Bernard became a priest. Bernadine's costume was bought from Poland. She had two different sizes. (CF.)

FLAYNA SADOWSKI. Daughter of Dr. and Mrs. Roman J. Sadowski, Flayna performed the Slavonic Rhapsody with the Polish Musical Institute of Art at the Belle Isle Shell during the Polish Festival. Her photograph ran in the *Detroit News*, and there were more than 3,000 people in attendance. (DNC/WRL.)

LAUR DANCERS, JULY 13, 1939. Polish dance groups are still active in Detroit today. They are sponsored by organizations such as Polish National Alliance and Polish Roman Catholic Union of America. There are over 20 groups in the metro area ranging from the Centennial Dancers, Gwiazda Dance School, PWA's Lowicz Dancers, and Rogalin Dance Troupe. Some use a region in their name such as Opole Dancers, Rzeszow Dancers, Tatry Dancers, and the Dunajec Song and Dance Ensemble. (DNC/WRL.)

ELEANOR ROOSEVELT'S VISIT, SEPTEMBER 9, 1935. Mrs. Franklin D. Roosevelt's visit to Detroit included the opening of the slum clearance project at 651 Benton Street. Her schedule was published in the *Detroit News*, and she was slated to watch the demolition from 3:05 to 3:25 p.m. From 3:30 to 4:00 p.m., she was to inspect the living conditions in the slum area and interview the residents. She was welcomed by a great number of ethnic groups throughout the day. (DNC/WRL.)

SOPHIA MIZERA. Mizera immigrated to Detroit from Poland in 1913. She married Vincent Lisowski in 1916, and in 1920, she brought her sisters Helen and Mary to the United States. Pictured in this Christmas 1926 photograph are, from left to right, Lucille Lisowska (Sophia's daughter), Helen Mizera Laba, Lottie Laba (Helen's daughter), Sophia Mizera Lisowska, Zigmund Lisowski (Sophia's son), and Helen Lisowska (Sophia's daughter). The photograph was taken in front of the carriage house in the Lisowski backyard on Thirtieth Street in Detroit. (JLS.)

PARADE, OCTOBER 7, 1928. East and Westsiders flocked to Hamtramck to celebrate. The *Detroit News* reported that 30,000 people gathered to celebrate the 10th anniversary of Polish independence. There was singing and dancing as well as a parade. Floats were featured in the parade, including this one with a boy dressed as the Polish white eagle and stretching his wings in freedom. (DNC/WRL.)

DEPRESSION ERA EVICTIONS, FEBRUARY 5, 1936. Many Poles faced difficult times during the Depression and some were evicted from their homes, like Andrew Lasobyk on Dubois Street. (DNC/WRL.)

PROHIBITION REPEALED, 1933. Celebrating the end of Prohibition, step-grandfather Thomas Stachelski is shown with his children and stepchildren in the backyard of the family home at 4128 Chene Street in the area around St. Albertus. (DS.)

PRUSS FARM OUTING, C. 1930. The Pruss family is pictured here visiting a relative's farm. William Pruss is in the foreground, Genevieve Pruss is on the far right, and Martha Pruss (née Chmielewski) is second from the right. (GPD.)

SACKA'S FARM, JULY 4, 1939. The Sacka farm truck appears here on July 4, 1939. Driving is John Sacka Sr. Sitting on the fender is his son Frank (nicknamed Sam) and on the running board is John Sacka Jr. They brought their fruit and vegetables to Western Market on Michigan and Eighteenth Street each Saturday morning from their farm in Romulus. In the afternoon, they would head to the Gasiorek house in Delray, where they would enjoy some good Polish food and spirits. (CGS.)

KRONK'S RECREATION. Frenchie and sisters Betty and Leona Przytulska pose after their recital at Olympia. They had taken dance classes at Kronk's Recreation—known more today for training boxers than dancers. Father Zadala scolded Betty for wearing the top hat and tails. Too Marlene Dietrich? (FEW.)

NEW YEAR'S, 1942. Walter Karakula leads the music on the concertina and drums. His repertoire of three tunes keeps the party going into the wee hours of the morning. The party was held in the basement of the Karakula's house on Central Avenue near Michigan Avenue. (TW.)

EASTOWN THEATER. The Eastown was one of Detroit's great neighborhood theaters. It opened originally in 1930 for the Wisper and Wetsman circuit. It was mainly a movie house, with a grand stage and large orchestra pit, which also hosted many of the finest stage shows in its early years. Depression-era giveaways at the theater included dishware. A whole set could be collected. (DNC/WRL.)

WOODWARD AVENUE, JULY 1, 1933. Shoppers flocked to the stores on Woodward. They would meet under the Kern's Clock, view the largest flag in the world at Hudson's, and shop for back-to-school clothes at Crowley Milner Company. A shopping spree would not be complete without a hot fudge sundae at Sanders. (DNC/WRL.)

96

STREET SNAPS, C. 1934. Chester Pruss is strolling down Woodward Avenue in Detroit in the vicinity of Campus Martius. (RP.)

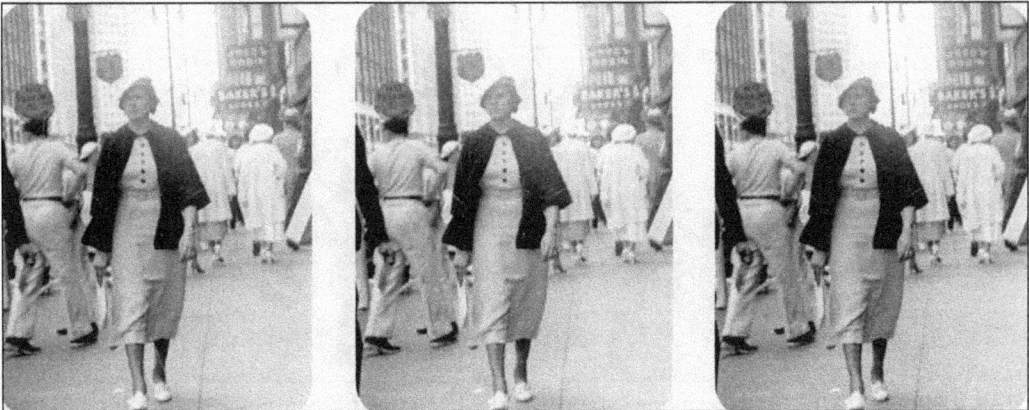

TRIPLE EXPOSURE. This candid photograph of Betty Przytulska near the Red Robin and Baker Shoe stores was typical of the 1930s. The shot was taken on Woodward and the street sign identifies it as Route 10, which was its highway number until 1970. The stamp on the back of the photograph advertises "Movie Flashes," Fox Theater, 829 Fox Theater Building, one six-by-eight-inch enlargement or three copies of these photographs cost 50¢. (FEW.)

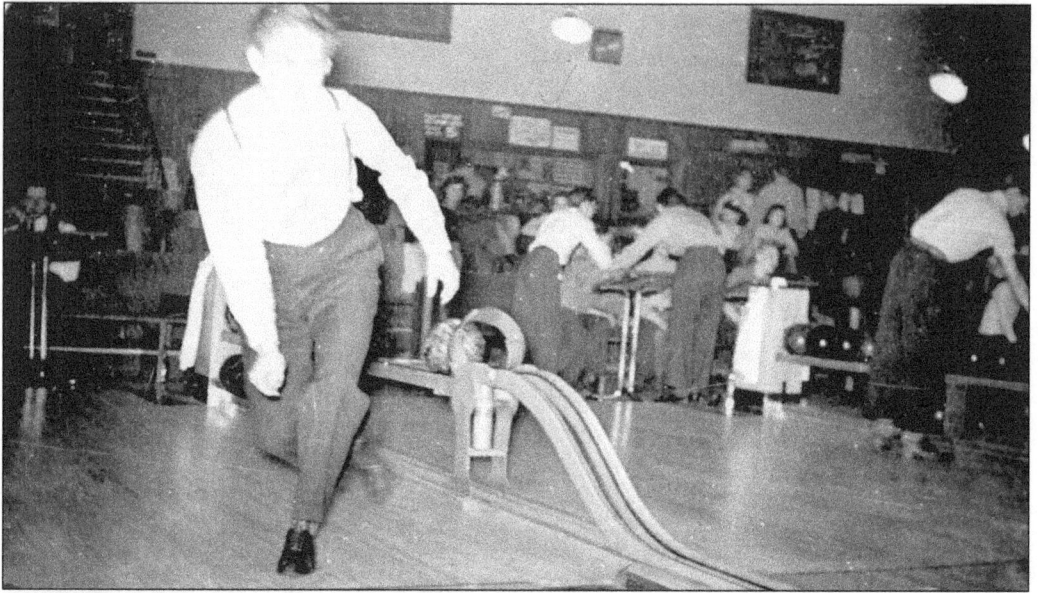

PATRICK'S FINE FORM, LATE 1930S. The photographer caught Patrick Topolewski's release of the ball. Patrick was an avid bowler from the 1930s well into the 1960s. He collected trophies for high game and most pins. (PFT.)

STAR TOOL AND DIE. Trying to bowl the perfect 300 game amid gutter balls, beer frames, and wax scoring pencils is bowling in Detroit! Moms and dads joined leagues sponsored by the parish, social clubs, or employers. Most carried their own bowling bag with a 16-pound ball and their personal bowling shoes. Here are bowlers in white shirts and ties from Starr Tool and Die at Hall Dodd's Recreation Center. John Voight is in the second row from the back, fifth bowler from the left (no tie). (JV.)

LORETTA BOTOROWICZ (WOZNIAK), 1937. Oh, to be 21 in 1937 with a good job at Burroughs Adding Machine and coworkers to join you in a friendly game of bowling. (TW.)

MIXED LEAGUE, 1943–1944. While some bowlers preferred a night out with just the guys or gals, this mixed league was sponsored by the Falcons Nest 939. The men agreed to shirts and ties, and the ladies detailed their uniforms with pocket hankies and hair ornaments. (CF.)

REFUGEES. There were 25 Polish war orphans between the ages of nine and eighteen. They were taken from their homes by Russian soldiers between 1939 and 1940 and sent to Siberia, where they did heavy labor for nearly two years. Gen. Wladyslaw Sikorski found a way to free 1,500 survivors, and they were sent to Teheran and, later, to India. They were given asylum at the Santa Rosa colony in Mexico. Then, after some time, they arrived at Guardian Angels Home, where they stayed for a few years. Seven years of flight and suffering ended. Programs of medical attention, rest, and entry into American schools and families prepared the girls and young woman to take up residence in foster-care homes. (AFSLM.)

Five

GROWING OLD
BUSIA, DZIADZIU, AND FAMILY PARTIES

PLAGENS 50TH ANNIVERSARY, 1927. The local newspaper announced, "Mr. and Mrs. Plagens celebrated their Golden Anniversary yesterday with services at the Assumption Catholic Church. The church was filled with relatives and friends of the old couple, and flowers of all sorts were given to the pair who were wed 50 years earlier. Later a reception was given at the home of relatives. Mrs. Plagens wept with joy at the reception given in her honor. Bishop Plagens, a nephew of Mr. M. Plagens led the church service." (LRD.)

MEN IN THE FAMILY, C. 1934. Pictured here is a joint family gathering of the Wojtkowiaks, Przytulskis, and Ewalds. Carl Henning, far right in the shadow, is holding a bottle of Goirke's Kashub Snuff. Next to him is Richard Topolewski. The fellow in front of Richard Topolewski is Steve Cebulski. The one with the white mustache is Jacob Ewald. Tony Przytulski is near Al Ewald in sunglasses, and John Voight is in the foreground. (FEW.)

SZYMANSKIS AND MORMOLS GATHER, 1938. Families with members who joined the convent will remember that visits home always meant bringing a companion. Here we see two Sisters of St. Joseph visiting the Szymanskis and Mormols. In 1889, Sisters of St. Joseph established a congregation at Kalamazoo, Michigan. The order had a hospital, a training school for nurses, a normal school, an orphan asylum, and several other educational institutions, besides supplying teachers for seven parish schools of the diocese. (BMV.)

ALL THE GIRLS, C. 1934. While the men of the family enjoyed a pinch of snuff, the women all seem to have a child in tow. The front line of squinting tots includes six girls and two boys. The moms include Anna Ewald Wroblewski and her sister Constance "Gustie" Ritter. The next woman is unknown, but in the center of the photograph is Lillian Ewald Lesinski with daughter Mildred. Over Lillian's right shoulder is Katherine Topolewski (with glasses). (FEW.)

AT 4738 RIOPELLE. Katherine (Kitty) Sitek's communion brought three generations together. The family gathers around grandmother Katherine Sitek (née Reczek). This photograph shows the size of the wooden houses along Riopelle. (CF.)

FOUR GENERATIONS, C. 1943. Genevieve Przytulska Benedetti (1916–1994) organized this studio photograph to document four generations. Mary Adamski Wojtkowiak Henning (1865–1952) is the matriarch. Her daughter Cecilia Wojtkowiak Pzytulska (1890–1977) lived on Beechdale down the street from her daughter Genevieve and her granddaughter Jacquelyn Benedetti (McEachran). The maternal line has longevity. Each mother back to 1753 has lived far past life expectancy. Using modern techniques their mt DNA has been determined to be H Haplogroup (with no mutations). It is 20,000 years old. (FEW.)

BACKYARD AT BANGOR AVENUE. While the kielbasa and sauerkraut or maybe *czarnina* simmered on the stove, Rose Voight hangs the laundry out to dry. The ritual was usually done on the same day each week, often with a bar of Fels Naptha laundry soap nearby. Laundry day was for the family, but many women earned pin money, or kept their family fed, by taking in laundry for rich people, that is anyone who could afford the service. Note the typical lot, narrow and deep, with the chicken coop, which would later become the garage near the alley. (JV.)

VENERABLE SOLANUS CASEY, 1870–1957. Patrick and Frances (Darling) Topolewski, Father Solanus Casey, Margaret Darling (Frances's mother), and her sister Mary Mulharen are pictured at the St. Bonaventure Monastery. Frances and Patrick visited Father Solanus several times before and after their wedding. This is a special family photograph from the Patrick Topolewski album. Father Solanus is being considered for sainthood. (PTF.)

Domzalski Celebration. This photograph commemorates the dual celebration of the family patriarch Michal Domzalski's 70th birthday and the 25th wedding anniversary of his son and daughter-in-law Walter "Jimmy" Domzalski and Mary Konkel Domzalski. Michal Domzalski was the first Polish insurance underwriter in Detroit. He was also a cofounder of the *Polish Daily News*. (KAM.)

STEPHEN OWIESNY FAMILY. The Stephen Owiesny family and the Drzewiecki family from Detroit are pictured here. Stephen Owiesny (1883–1971) arrived in the United States in 1902 from the village of Wola, Klecko, Posen. His wife Marianna Drzewiecka (1886–1964) is a first generation Pole who lived her entire life in Detroit's Poletown area and was the niece of Thomas Zoltowski, King of the Poles. This picture was taken at the Owiesny residence on East Warren Avenue in Detroit. (DBO.)

MERIQUE AND CIESLIGA WEDDING. This is the wedding photograph of Margaret Rose Merique and Alfred Louis Ciesliga, taken on August 20, 1949. Their grandmothers were gathered for this family portrait. From left to right they are Helena Hubner Lark (1879–1958), Otillia Wagner Merique (1869–1951), Anastasia Ceranska Ciesliga (1885–1955), and Paulina Baran Darga (1869–1960). (KAM.)

FROM MÜHLBANZ TO DETROIT. Franz Wendt (1837–1908) and his wife Paulina Stelmach Wendt (1835–1918) were the last family members to come to Detroit from Kreis Dirschau. They were preceded by their son Franz, who saved enough money to bring his parents and siblings, Adolph and Julianna, to Michigan. Franz died in 1908, and his wife Paulina died in 1918. They were buried at Mount Olivet Cemetery in Detroit. (FEW.)

RODZINA PRZYTULA, C. 1896. The Przytula (Przytulski) family followed the typical sequence of migration. First the single son, Mikolaj (Nicolas), came to the United States, followed by his father, Adam. Mikolaj earned a $1 a day and saved enough to pay for the passage of his mother, sister, and nephew in 1896. Poles said they wanted to come to America where there were sausages on every fence. Looks like Johana, Adam, Mikolaj, and Stanislawa await delivery at their home on Lovett. Johana (1842–1905) and Adam (1837–1914) are buried at Holy Cross Cemetery in Detroit. (FEW.)

WESOLYCH SWIAT, MERRY CHRISTMAS, 1945. Mary Samull decorated the tree in this photograph. The family always had a large, live tree, which was often bought at the Eastern Market. A crèche and Christmas village were under the tree, often occupying even up to a quarter of the room's floor space. Many ornaments were made of paper, and aluminum icicles filled the tree. Christmas Eve was always meatless. (DS.)

ALFRED Z. WOZNIAK, 1942. This photograph was taken while he was dating Loretta Botorowicz either on Williams Street or East Milwaukee. They got married on Tuesday, which happened to be D-day, June 6, 1944. Alfred never had problems remembering his anniversary. (TW.)

Six

ETERNAL REST
CEMETERY VISITS

BODY OF PRIEST LIES IN STATE, FEBRUARY 17, 1903. The *Detroit Free Press* reported on page 1 that "The remains of Rev. Jozef Dabrowski lay in state at St. Albertus's church last night and were viewed by thousands of the deceased's countrymen. The church was draped in mourning and bier was heaped with floral offerings. Members of the various societies connected with the church knelt in prayer before the body of their benefactor." (AFSLM.)

CORTÈGE OF REV. FRANCIS A. MUELLER, APRIL 23, 1913. The *Detroit News* reported, "At 10:30 the process of acolytes, monks, priests and laymen and women, representatives of the various sodalities of the church, moved to the rectory to escort the body. Shortly after 11 o'clock, the deep tolling of the bells in the steeple announced its approach and the hush of deep prayer came over the entire assemblage. Led by a cross bearer and candle bearers the procession moved slowly from the rectory. The Christian Mothers's sodality headed by its banner headed the cortège. Following came the societies of St. Stanislaus, St. Albertus, St. Joseph, the Blessed Trinity, SS. Peter and Paul, St. Martin, St. Hyacinth, St. Valentine, the Sacred Heart, Catholic Order of Foresters, C.M.B.A., L.C.B.A., the Young Ladies sodality and the Third Order of Saint Francis, all in full regalia of their uniforms and each order headed by its banner bearers. The line of priests in official garb bore the rich mahogany casket, impressive in its simplicity." (DNC/WRL.)

FRANCISZEK KRUPINSKI. This tombstone photograph was taken by Bill Gorski in the early 1980s, when the tombstone was intact. The cemetery record now indicates the cross had been vandalized and is broken. Franciszek was born March 6, 1851, and died May 3, 1898. He is interred at Sacred Heart Cemetery in the old north section ND, row five, headstone six. (JWG.)

FRANCISZKA DIEBAL, 1878–1904. Franciszka's cemetery records list her tombstone as a cement cross. She was born October 9, 1879, and died in Detroit on May 6, 1904. Her grave is in the section NE, row seven, headstone three. Other Diebal burials include August, section CK, row 12, headstone 21. Edward and Victoria Diebal have two headstones in section CL, row 11, headstones six and eight. All are interred at Sacred Heart Cemetery. (JWG.)

PRAYING FOR THE DEAD. Here the Felician Sisters pray at Fr. Jozef Dabrowski's grave. Catholics receive partial indulgence when they pray for the souls in purgatory by devoutly visiting a cemetery and praying for the departed, even if the prayer is only mental. A plenary indulgence can be gained each day between November 1 and 8. In the Detroit area, the following cemeteries have many Polish interments: Holy Cross, Holy Sepulchre, Mount Olivet, Mount Elliott, St. Hedwig, and Sacred Heart. "Eternal rest grant to them, O Lord, and let perpetual light shine upon them. May the souls of the faithful departed, through the mercy of God, rest in peace. Amen." (AFSLM.)

AS THE STORM UNHEEDED BLEW, FEBRUARY 18, 1903. The *Detroit News* reported on page 5 that "In a blizzard that piled the snow in huge drifts around the monuments and tombstones of Mt. Elliott, the mortal remains of Rev. Jozef Dabrowski was today laid to rest. Not since the funeral of Fr. Kolasinski, five years ago, had there been such an outpouring of people as attended the funeral held at St. Albertus church. The church was in deep mourning, with streamers of black wound from pillar to pillar far down the aisles to the chancel rail." (AFSLM.)

SISTERS VISIT MOUNT ELLIOTT CEMETERY. On the 50th anniversary of the death of Father Dabrowski, the Felician Sisters prayed and placed a commemorative wreath at his grave. (AFSLM.)

KONKELS, SIDE BY SIDE. Catherine (1882–1935) and Telef/Teofil (1882–1977) are shown here at rest. The family lived at 563 Grandy Street in 1920 with their children, Marie, Edward, and Helen. By 1930, the street numbers changed and their home was listed as 5412 Grandy Street. Edward had joined his father as an autoworker. They are interred at Sacred Heart Cemetery. (JWG.)

PIOTR BERNATOWICZ (1894–1935). The family changed their surname to Bernatt. He is buried at Sacred Heart Cemetery. His wife, Mary, was buried at his side. (JWG.)

SITEK. Maryanna Sitek (1851–1935), wife of John, came from Galicia in 1884 and had nine children. Four children were living with them at 261 Alexandrine Street in 1900. Stanislaw, Joseph, Frank, Annie, and Sofia. Stanislaw was born in Poland, and the younger siblings were born in Michigan. Maryanna was living with her daughter Sofia and son-in-law Josef Machowski in 1920 at 575 Medbury Street. Photographed at Sacred Heart Cemetery in 1983, the tombstone today is missing the portrait and cross. (JWG.)

OTILIA (1871–1941) AND JOSEPH A. BOLDA (1864–1928). In 1920, the family lived at 92 Hale with daughter Mary. Joseph could read and write and was born in West Prussia. He was employed in the shipyards. He was naturalized in 1885. They are interred at Sacred Heart Cemetery. (JWG.)

117

GRANDMA. Franziska Eugenia Pruss (née Zolkowski) is lying in repose on May 22, 1922, in Detroit. She was born on June 16, 1857, in Laskownica, Schubin, Posen. She immigrated to the United States from Wagrowiec, Poland, with her husband, Walenty Pruss, in April 1882 on the steamship *Braunschweig* out of Bremen, Germany. She was the mother of William, Steven, Michael, Joseph, Philip, Antoinette, Bernard, and Mary Pruss. While Polish undertakers prepared the deceased for burial, most wakes took place in the home. A white wreath on the door indicated the death of a child, a black wreath the death of an adult. The Pruss parlor is traditionally decorated with a picture of a name day saint, a custom brought with them from Poland. Another piece of funerary tradition is placing a clock in the floral arrangement, set to the time that the person died. (GPD.)

SZCZEPAN (STEPHEN) GLOD, JUNE 2, 1941. Stephen was a talented musician and played five instruments. He was born April 11, 1884, in Jasionka, Krosno, Podkarpackie. He came to America in 1903. He married Rozalia Cislo on October 8, 1906, at the Sacred Heart Church in Braddock, Pennsylvania. They had 10 children. Rozalia (born on September 9, 1883) died on August 24, 1964. Stephen is buried in Mount Olivet Cemetery in Detroit, and Rozalia is buried in Forest Lawn Cemetery in Detroit. (JT.)

EMILIA, 1910–1931. The Szweczyk tombstone commemorates Emilia and her parents, Ludwika and Stanislaw. The graves are in the central section of Sacred Heart Cemetery, section CL, row six, headstone seven. She was born September 15, 1910, and died December 23, 1931. (JWG.)

GASIOR. The Gasior family headed by John and Katherine included their six children living at 26 Osborne Place in 1920. John was an autoworker and daughter Marian worked in a cigar factory. As of 1930, John had not become a United States citizen. They are interred at Sacred Heart Cemetery. (JWG.)

EMILIA SZWECZYK (1910–1931). The Szweczyk family lived at 3407 Harper Street. The parents arrived in the United States in 1901. Emilia was the middle of five children. They were a typical automobile-industry family. She was a stenographer for an automobile company. Her younger sister Eleanor made cushions at the factory. Father Stanley was a construction foreman, and brother John worked on the assembly line. They are buried at Sacred Heart Cemetery. (JWG.)

MARIE AND ANTONI PISKOROWSKI. Antoni arrived at Castle Garden in 1881 and is listed in the 1890 Detroit City Directory living at 780 Riopelle Street. He worked as a varnisher and is interred at Sacred Heart Cemetery. Marie (June 16, 1880–November 8, 1952) and Antoni (November 2, 1875–April 10, 1919) are buried in a family plot. Other burials include Franciszka and Antoni, Frank J. and Marie M. Piskorowski, section CL, row seven. (JWG.)

UNKNOWN TOMBSTONE PORTRAIT. She will always be fresh and young in her photograph. Did the family select a photograph of the departed in her Easter bonnet or standing up to a wedding? She is interred at Sacred Heart Cemetery. (JWG.)

UNKNOWN TOMBSTONE PORTRAIT. The portrait brings to mind a young woman posing for a engagement photograph or a young mother marking a special occasion. She is interred at Sacred Heart Cemetery. (JWG.)

122

UNKNOWN TOMBSTONE PORTRAIT.
The selected portrait seems to
convey a sassy sense of humor and
vitality. Did she have naturally curly
hair, or did she use a curling iron to
achieve the marcel? She is interred
at Sacred Heart Cemetery. (JWG.)

UNKNOWN TOMBSTONE PORTRAIT.
The portrait recalls Jean Harlow and a bit
of Joan Blondell. Photographic tombstones
originated in France in 1854 but were
popularized by southern Europeans. This
working-class art form was adopted by the
Poles throughout the state of Michigan and
has been documented by Pam Lazar and
photographed by Bill Gorski. She is interred
at Sacred Heart Cemetery. (JWG.)

REV. DOMINICK H. KOLASINSKI. Founder and pastor of the Sacred Heart of Mary's Church in Detroit, Kolasinski was born in Mielec, Galicia, on August 3, 1838. He died April 11, 1898, and was buried at Sacred Heart Cemetery. He came to America in 1882 in order to assume the pastorate of St. Albertus Church in Detroit. He was removed from the pastorate on November 28, 1885, without being given due cause. His removal led to seven major Polish riots in Detroit. (JWG.)

KOLASINSKI COMES BACK TO DETROIT. Kolasinski returned to Detroit on December 8, 1888. His followers had already begun a parochial school in August 1886 at 4455 Riopelle Street. This was the beginning of Sacred Heart of St. Mary Parish, later known as Sweetest Heart of Mary Parish. Kolasinski became the leader of Sweetest Heart of Mary Parish, which had been excommunicated from the Diocese of Detroit. Kolasinski and his parish were received into the fold of the Roman Catholic Church in Detroit on February 18, 1894. (JWG.)

UNKNOWN TOMBSTONE PORTRAIT.
The portrait could easily have been
from a graduation or a wedding.
He will eternally be handsome
and healthy. He is interred at
Sacred Heart Cemetery. (JWG.)

UNKNOWN TOMBSTONE PORTRAIT.
The military portrait captures
the soldier at the height of his
youth and vigor. He is interred at
Sacred Heart Cemetery. (JWG.)

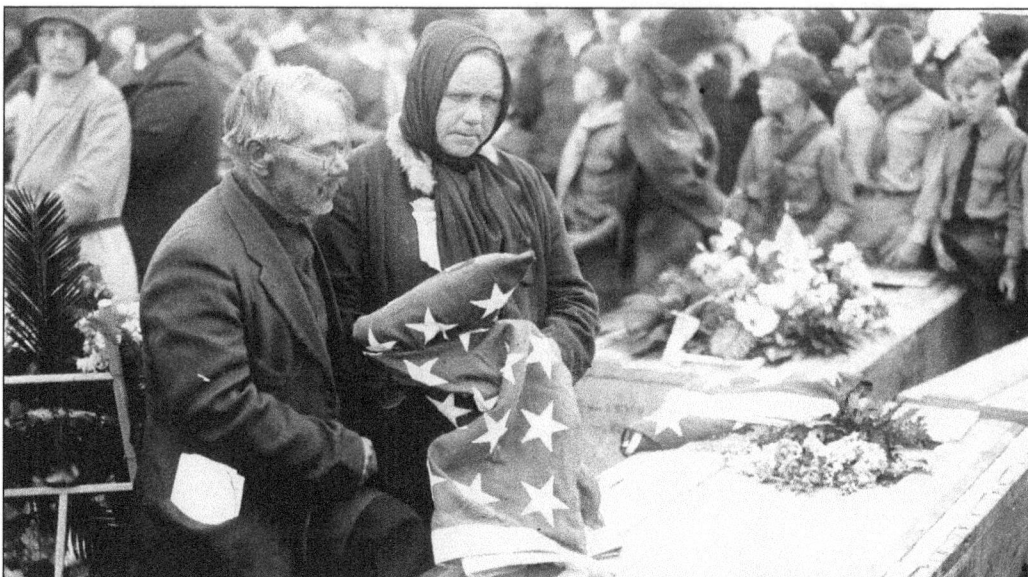

FUNERAL FOR THE FALLEN, 1930. Pictured here is the 339th Infantry Regiment at White Chapel Cemetery. The war had been over for nearly 12 years, but some families did not see their sons return home until 1930. Known as the "Polar Bears," the unit spent the duration of the war in Siberia. Mr. and Mrs. Frank Skocelas, parents of Pvt. Andrew Skocelas, receive the casket and flag of their son. (DNC/WRL.)

MEMORIAL DAY. Each year descendants gather at White Chapel Cemetery in Troy, Michigan, where the remains of soldiers of the 339th Infantry Regiment that were first buried in Russia are interred. The burial monument is striking, with a black granite base topped by a large white marble Polar Bear. Interment around the monument includes Max Kurowski, Joseph Kalaski, Joseph Marchlewski, and Leo Sajnaj. John Voight is front and center. (JV.)

MAZIASZ. Son Felix (1887–1923), mother Antonina (1859–1949), and father Joseph (1849–1923) are interred at Sacred Heart Cemetery. This photograph is part of the series Bill Gorski began in the 1980s to photograph the Polish tombstone portraits throughout the state of Michigan. (JWG.)

FELIX MAZIASZ, 1887–1923. Pictured here is a close-up of the portrait of Felix Maziasz. (JWG.)

RONNIE AND JOEY HARDECKI, C. 1940S. The grandsons of Ludwika Kwarciak Suchyta visit her grave site. Louise was born on January 23, 1883, and died from complications of childbirth on October 27, 1926. She was first interred at Holy Cross Cemetery and then moved to Mount Hope in Allen Park when her husband was buried. (CGS.)

www.ingramcontent.com/pod-product-compliance
Lightning Source LLC
Chambersburg PA
CBHW080620110426
42813CB00006B/1561